BEAUTIFUL VEINS
POEMS BY
JOSEPH SHERMAN

THE ACORN PRESS
CHARLOTTETOWN
2006

Beautiful Veins
ISBN 1-894838-20-3
© 2006 by Joseph Sherman

Editing: David Helwig
Cover photo: "Far Away" by M. Green
Design: Matthew MacKay
Printing: Hignell Book Printing

The Acorn Press gratefully acknowledges the support of the Prince Edward Island Council of the Arts and the Cultural Affairs Division of the PEI Department of Community and Cultural Affairs.

Library and Archives Canada Cataloguing in Publication
Sherman, Joseph, 1945–2006.
 Beautiful veins / Joseph Sherman.
Poems.
ISBN 1-894838-20-3
 I. Title.
PS8587.H386B42 2006   C811'.54   C2006-900366-1

ACORNPRESS

The Acorn Press
P.O. Box 22024
Charlottetown, Prince Edward Island
Canada C1A 9J2

www.acornpresscanada.com

For Beatrice, Rebekah, and Matthew Sherman
and for Ann Sherman
with love

contents

"far away" 1955

This is me without his glasses on. This is him
wearing my best striped summer jersey.

The opened book is a *Golden Treasury* volume with sharp gilt edges,
the brass candlestick is from a grandfather's dining room,
and the heightened flame... a forged future,
or so we think to have thought.

There is no certitude in it or in the boy's flame-lit face
worked to scale through avuncular instruction
(the photographer uncle), a transitive face, its expression
ordered up as enigmatic—still,
still one life with all the promise of its beautiful veins.

BLACK AND RUST
For Don Domanski

I laughed to cry when Don elected black and rust.
Wear the Pier colours proudly, I'd humoured
as he headed off to Banff. The Pier colours...

And as we are the two of us Pier Dears
—that's Whitney Pier, the once-hardhatted
purlieu of Sydney, Cape Breton, Nova Scotia,
where battle pennons have always been appropriate—
I could dab some grey on our flag of convenience,
recalling new snow peppered over a one-night shift
of blast furnace and coke-ovened hours.

But I also remember the sky, what filled it.
With young lungs we sucked all in, didn't we,
Don? He's a poet, out to Banff.

No great seal for the plaintiffs of a Whitney Pier
gone tarry with eco-grief, its choral choking
slurried, but a vision in my now peppery head of a new
rag of a flag, its colours black and rust and raised
so high from the shop and valley floor,
one must restore, to cheer or weep.

OLD PHOTO OF TWO BROTHERS IN UNIFORM

The youngest of twelve,
Yeshiel chooses to remain near Grodno
with his weak lungs,
though perhaps he has no choice;
it is difficult to know
ninety years on.

He is ill-at-ease
in the Czar's military issue,
you could tell, I can tell.

And rumour prevails
that he may have died wearing it,
or shortly after removing it
for the last time.

· · ·

His older brother,
my great-uncle Aaron-Leib,
demobilized, will live to be a family man,
receiving parcels of dry goods and tinned edibles
from his siblings, faraway immigrants
in havenish Canada.

He will long be out of uniform,
his moustaches shorn, when
White Russia goes ignescent in 1941,
and the care packages slide into a void.

Of the two who remained behind,
Yeshiel is the lucky one.

early scan

The human voice prepares me
for the inhuman, instructs
that I might pose,
                    display,
reveal,
          says
the dye is colourless
and will make me go warm.

Human hands adept
at tube-twisting,
                    at aiming
the nibbed needle,
signal
        for my stillness.

The catafalque is brightly
lit,
    a cylinder
into which I am slid
beneath the decimals
by which I am claimed.

Hold your breath,
orders the inhuman voice.
Then, breathe.

The cylinder surrounds
these moments—the metallic
words, an acridity within,
a vein song of heat.

Be slid.

Be still.

Breathe in.

Out.

FATHER'S DAY GRUEN (2005)

Seconds count for nothing
now, only
      minutes,
           hours,
               days.

A life creeps
rich and golden
past this
blackened face of time.

THE FAKE BIRTHDAY

David is having a fake birthday
at our house—his sixth—and solemnly
informs us so, even as he confirms that
yes we have presents. "Do you have balloons?"
he asks solemnly as well, and no we do not.

"For your fake seventh birthday," I buoy him.

Today he is that rarity, the little gentleman,
awash with information, and prompt to say thank you.
I am suspicious and relieved. He has been
a poster child for the out-of-control, his sisters
lamblike observers, but today
they are ill or rebellious and must be palliated,
even as David impresses us with possibility.

He will be six in another week, but his fake
birthday is what we hope he will remember.

TWO FROM CAPE TRYON

Wonders at the Cape

Upon seeing for the first time
a stone sea serpent—
there is a benediction

Upon learning that this stone sea serpent,
(its forbidding face resembling that of my father)
preyed upon U-boats and their evil captains,
a lifetime and a half ago—
a benediction

Upon observing
a soloing cormorant claim cliff
and painted serpent's back
in a threading motion,
in service to a supple needle—
a benediction

Upon seeing wary travelers
from a distant land (parents,
a brace of children, a growling mutt)
camped upon the cape, witnesses to
serpent and seabird, and black-winged
butterflies circling Eden—
give thanks

Upon stumbling into nameless flowers
beneath the imprecise flight of
the black-winged butterflies,
and within earshot of the brooding creatures—
a quiet prayer

Upon observing a fishing boat far below,
sea-anchored and shadowed by the cliffs,
its adult male occupants swaying in afternoon prayer

and instructing a beardless boy,
still tucking his fringed garment beneath his oilskins,
in the praise-words that inspire the cormorants
to gape and soar—
a hosanna

Upon reviewing the nature of love
and the working of love behind
the stony vigil of the guardian serpent,
and within earshot
of visitors earthbound and airborne—
this prayer

Upon stirring the red dirt atop
the lighthouse road that leads to and from
this washboard sea and its denizens,
morning, noon, eve—
this perfervidity

Upon electing not to broadcast
certain secrets, but to claim what
one loves and hoard and guard it
and speak on it only in loving riddles—
repeat these blessings three times.

Odd Man Over

Word has reached us
of the poet said to have plunged
from the P.E.I. headland,
over the cliff unobserved
but imagined in downward flight
halted by the rocky shore at slack-tide
(a blessing, he can't swim),
shattering both wrists and ankles,
though not his melon head.

Night falls late
in the month of Av,

the cormorants barely shifting
as they edge into sleep,
even the stone sea serpent
a composed neighbour
in the breaker-rent dark.

The poet's people learn of the fall,
first from above, then
from the lifting sea, upon which
a pitching lobster boat heaves to,
crewed by serious greybeards
who take him off gently
at the pleasure of time and tide,
keening to themselves religiously
(an old salt's device),
as his screams pepper the dark,
the boat's thrub beating through the pain.

Two hours before
he had claimed the cape,
facing first the shadow-strewn fields,
then the Quebec sea, made denser
by the whispers from below,
no place
for an artist with a low threshold
for news of the unknown.

His last conscious thought, then,
now help's arrived, on a rope, on a boat,
is one for convalescence,
every prospect named,
before his stranger's life is named,
in chorus, by men
who would deny, if addressed,
that one brought so low could be so fervent.

He'd been reciting the evening prayers,
says his tearful father into a microphone—
Thank the Lord he'll live to repeat them.

TWO WeaTHeR Poems

Charlottetown Cenotaph
12 November 2000

Beneath the uncompromising rain
the effulgent plastic poppies
speak eloquently to eternal life.

The Centre Does Not Hold in March

A burning mortgage lights up
the sky.
          In its glow
I finger the spruce and metal
apparatus of a skunk trap—
consider the dead sparrowhawk.

HER WAITING ROOM

I am late with this.
                The moment
there was a question
there was meant to be
a response,
          a mélange of words
adding up to something like
their singular worth. This is
the price tag of panic,
the lyric spine of fear—

I know yours, the betrayal
you feel knotting within you,
the mystery with no measure
of charm.

          But what of me?
I must consider. And keep watch.
Nothing will comfort
but your own release.

This is when
every gesture counts, more
than any order of words, when
whatever I might do for you
must come as one breath,
then the next,
and the next.

From the moment
the match was struck,
I did nothing but place
one foot before the other
until a destination loomed.

I was supposed to know
that other language, to learn
what I do not know,
what now fails to arm me,
and my voice was to spill out
in that wordless song, some
renegade priest's perfect prayer—

my body, with yours,
end one waltz and cue another.

WHEN PAIN MUST BE GOOD

Pain must be good when mystery defines it,
or at least lends it a cast.

You fly awake in the darkest
hour (to date), writhing,
wondering whether to wake
your partner, seek higher help,

wondering if it is too late,
if this agony in your left thigh
will consume you
and never leave a name.

Doesn't need to,
you are bestowing identity.
Raw sound efforms from behind your lips,
fingers tendril—
a dumb red thought
                          reaching out.

a poem out of Pete

For long I thought to know
I shouldn't spurn him so
but make him into literature...

For Pete called my women names
and stole my logs, stealthily,
kvetching to my face
how hard it'd been to heft and
pitch them over the fence between,
one January night,
and he with a broken arm besides.

"You can take them things back,
if you choose," he barked at me,
rocking on his doorstep,
"They're too piss-green to chop or burn."

Yes, that's a proper cue for laughs,
and, in hindsight, a salute to rude
grit and gumption
and the passion to scavenge and hoard
that was Pete's life, as neighbour.

He warred with a raucous son
over the junk he claimed from
curbsides across town and hauled home,
trailed for years by Kaya, his Samoyed,
who ate cats, Pete unmoved.

There was the time he'd have had me
help him shift his junk from the curb
where the son had consigned it,
back to the pile propping up his side
of the shared fence,

Pete, who ought to have been recorded,
keening a cappella the country blues
songs his brainpan retained
and recycled through his nose,
years after the infamous cellar tumble
taken at work
that sent him home to his invisible leash.

Day and night a bony frame might
bend into an Island breeze,
might be found three miles away, leaning,
or laconically ambling,
homing instinct on hold.

He died not a year past
his silent wife's final silence,
of a cancer he never addressed—
there'd been fewer tunes of late
scrawling the night air.

His last neighbourhood tour, truncated—
a night crawl across the far neighbour's lawn
to say he was hurting,
guessed he'd best see the docs.

And my last image—the week before,
of a millworker's hat riding
that dance of bones in greyed denim,
aiming an unsteady bike down our street,

to be driven past,
not a glance in my distorting mirror.

UNIT 731
(LIMITS OF THE HUMAN BODY) 1943–45

What wonders might not emerge, as
though from a besmirched chrysalis, if sober men
out of Japanese science and of highest repute
are given their way with human guinea pigs
made captive in a northern land

where the Hippocratical and the humane vapourize
with the risen sun, and the sole anointed
are such doctors and warders—serious men,
grim players in the great and lesser waiting game—
this war's addenda being theirs to swim.

Typhus, dysentery, bubonic plague, cholera
all names on a prescribed list, now thinned syrups
for a syringe, pustules on the skin, pain,
questions caught in an inexorably closing throat—
what happens next

in Manchukuo where, among its ghostly inhabitants,
one Chinese emperor, last of his breed, a Japanese
captive here on earth, shares a silken palace
(no experiment) with a drug-addict empress
and a concubine who wears school uniforms.

So much commingled madness and sobriety,
this world of knowledge farced by dissonance,
with pails awash in riven rules—
a theatre for the machinations of those
who would cure war's many prisoners of hope, the disease.

"a monument to terror"

This is all that is left... (AFP Photo caption)

I've been saving this stark photo on newsprint,
beautiful in its fated and fading authenticity,
echoed in the national journals of many nations
days after its subject matter was hewn,
sculpted by a ruder metal
and cured in a flame fed by the highest octane.

When I registered this cuticular slice
of a cathedral of commerce slid down through the sky,
I declaimed to the multitude that this could be jewelry,
this, in miniature, a striking/stricken brooch,
to be replicated and purveyed.

Three years on I still think so and perhaps
it's been done; the heavens know there remain
many cathedrals of commerce.

This brittle clipping is artefact, soon to be
as yellow as bones left cooling, after
the hunter's blade has spoken its mantra...

The truth in this photograph:
what I see when I study it, without
the acrid evident in my nose and mouth,
without the cut and roar assailing my ears,
remains terrible and beautiful both, safely so,
as if a certain old poem holds comfortably
as prophecy and commentary.

Death can never be old news so long
as painted new, so long as we call the earth
a page, a canvas, receptive to all that descends—
here, a small town rained down.

Art is beauty—another and older sentiment.
Perfect in gracing the perfect lapel. A good cause.
I see this in silver brocade.

I've been saving this stark photo,
as an innocent might some remnant blossoms
marking an old season, its petals secured
between the pages of a new silence.
This is all that is left.

I SPY A TRILOBITE

We are nothing
in geologic time
if not creatures who have
outgrown their wings

dismissing the jewelry
stored in amber houses

saying yes to the dawn
when there's no ounce of blood
left to squeeze from the sky.

THE ESQUIRE'S TALE

Uncle Tott would say to purchase land,
preferably scrub near a creek
or in the lee of a barrow,
though he never bought a scrap himself
but took to let his entire life

a caravan plot dappled with silver eggs,
during those middle years
past sundering his affaires d'amour,
and wedlock with the ripe Miranda.

Nor did the youngsters purchase,
nary an acre, though all four knew
the old man craved vindication
through diminished lives,
their efforts

and what remained unattainable
hung as invisible weights
from an old cross borne,
that floating cabin swiped by the tide.

Uncle Tott saved himself
a hill of many pennies,
dusting with shadows the sign reading
Sold

that spoke so plainly of rank,
authority, the bedeviling glory
in all of false promise.

A simple gesture, that Amen
in the nation of Commerce.
This land is my land.

FANCY'S FRONT PARLOUR:
THE LIVING ROOM SUITE

Bay Window

Naked now your cushions
are gone, your faux-lattices
slap against streaked glass,
sculpture nestles in your white lap.

There are Quebec influences, South African,
but that's another poem. In a bad story

the view you afford, in or out, would be an illusion,
reality an impermeable fog shouldering up
against a mirror of window panes,
the house diminishing
the nearer guests get
to their greeting.

Art on the Wall

There are eleven prints and paintings
on the L-shaped walls
and I call them after their makers,
so these are lady paintings:
Erica, Hilda, Daphne, Wendy, Carol, Colleen.
None of them is Jewish.
Only the boy painting, Neil.

I Lied

Some of them are guys,
some of the art is masculine
(the sculpture both),
not all Jewish, hardly religious
at all.

Fireplace

Useless monster, we
turn to you in the cold,
a maw in a skull of stone—
devouring, gossiping smoke.

Heintzman

My grandmother bought it
used, for furniture at least,
or to be played unseasonably
as meteors fall.

The key that's succumbed
to the unexpected, unknown
to me, hides its note
among the yellowed teeth
of our ancestors.

Old Leather Chair and Cat

Both prove to be brown beneath
the light thrown by the glass of pretense
rather than the black of their seeming,

and both command the room,
taking charge, racing to fill the spaces
between the far points of

this domestic compass, caged
by colour shifting with each
opening of either door,

welcoming the weather
leather fur four legs chair brass teeth...
meow or better yet that glance.

English Hand Bell

The blue Devonian bird roosting
its ceramic bell does not sing,
the clapper makes a tuneless thunk—
aesthetics ring proudly,
defend their territory.

A Pair of Figurative Blue Wedgwood Plaques

Priceless—which is
to say that Bob had them
valued once, in Stoke,
a year before he fell.

A Peter Thomas

Though this is a production pot,
a no-handle spouted grip-pitcher
for cream, gravy, lemon curd,
its shape and glaze-locked colours
speak so yellow fine to this eye
I had to quick-draw my Royal Crown reticule.

Stained Carpet

Soup, crumb sets, assorted
sauces, cat bile and cat hair
beneath our feet and gaze—
guests avert theirs, find
the cracks in our ceiling.

Mussel and Feather

This boat model, what they call
a half-model, mined out of dark varnish,
its Welsh layers a feast for the eye
once again, in a way
Ann's Great-Uncle's Mussel might,
in Abersoch Harbour, approximate,

the contemporary found feather
commanding our anchoring chain—
boat to wall of life.
    A way of saying
you can be serious,
crow.

A Walter Ostrom

Its flaw, one paler than pale yellow tulip
embellishing this elliptical vase of all vases
with its grid lid, is seen as a grace note
to the busy perfection of imperfection, and so
does a contingent of delphiniums belong here,
each stem displayed with pert authority—
this the glory of the turtle-shelled lid of holes,
the genius of the making and the relegation
to retail and the appreciative possessor
of a ceramic master's take-it-or-leave-it.

The Silent Piano

The silent piano platforms
seventeen photographs,
black and white, sepia, colour,
of strangers who are friends,
family, three generations
caught in dusty timelock.

A piano moment
this cliché, the what-ifs,
the raging recollection
of tough musical futures.

Sculpture

Two pieces only,
Le Temple is Jewish,
monolithic, dense and striated
as Quebec marble.

The other is mounted bronze
of a lesser and a greater palm or face
facing, really a casting miniature,
sentimental, a plaintive

attempt to celebrate
maternity, the mythical serenity
of hard conjoinings.

Tea Bowls

Two are mine, two are Ann's,
all are made by Tom Smith.
You know tea bowls,
how dear they are in Japan,
what a bargain these must seem,

however hot they become
when a well of boiling water
and terre verte leaves,
almost too much heat to hold,

so now sit in the south window
with a smelt-sucking Royal Copenhagen Kingfisher
and a man blown out of cool blue glass.

C'est ça

I can't write of everything,
but wish to assure you
that there is more
and that this is only the poem.

Piano Bench

No more bottom, where
do we store the sheet music,
the sad magazines?

Black Floor Lamp

Hot-pepper halogen bulb,
the one luminescence in a deceptively long room,
rooted, sculpturally modernist—
a metallic phallic pillar
tippable but lovely light
switch slid on or off.

Alex Livingston's Mouse

This disheveled rodent, an arch-image
lifted from some naturalist's tome
had its time as a shelf-mounted painting
(in emulation of an etching) before
being re-mounted over the downstairs bif,
where mainly erudite men address
his scabrous charms. We study his lines,
for he is worth each effort; such is art by Alex—
this literary mouse, once lost among our bookshelves.

1663

Forty-seven years after Shakespeare's death
the pieces of this chest were carved,
assembled, and sold to a Welsh milliner
whose name is immaterial,
unlike the woodwork.

History has become, in languishing
here amidst Canadian tears,
a legacy to the literate—
otherwise antique money,
current taste, kindling.

Neil's Windows *Painting*

I'd heard he's had cancer,
the artist. A pity.
This lovely and luminous
oil ingress shows so much,
if little enough of what is.

Brass Cauldron on its Side

Sometimes home to
a plush mallard,
sometimes a nest
to rarefied air, floor
children breathing.

King Charles Spaniels

Parenthesizing a shelf
collection of lustre-wear
above the west window,
oblivious to their seasons,
the porcelain deceits.

Two Processional Candlesticks from Britain

Swag.

Moulded Deity

I believe he giggled as he
unpacked Krishna the souvenir,
but then he is the baby scion
of a wealthy plutocrat,
a veritable Prince, if unwise.

We are the hosts we are,
with our dusty shelves
and our knowing smiles—
waiting for our Ganesha.

Sweetgrass Sewing Basket

Betty's, bought at
a yard sale after
her death.

A steatite loon nests
the lid, proud
as a hood ornament—
our threads now stored within.

Wendy Kindred

Does woodcuts for her own
tidy books, this painting
from a series for America's
Bicentennial.

Northern Maine. *Pink Field.*
There's late-winter white and there's a hopeful pale blue.
Flat as life itself.
Eliciting questions.
Epiphanies.
A first.
$60.

Ethel Rosenfeld's Le Temple

What would we compare this to,
were the Sphinx not part
of my lexicon.
your legacy?

Lazy Boy

The new recliner's embrace is never
entire, and allows for some
exhaled contemplation of
the alternative to its firm grip
of ancient dollar-green leather—
impervious, in my mind of need,
to dreck and spillage, including
that of my own staunchless ichor.

Above the Hearth

Floyd's red poster (now)
replaces the anonymous
Welsh landscape
strung on a hook
above our fireplace—

his postage-stamp rendering
of RW, that Righteous Gentile
from whom I've pressed indulgence,
risking smoke above stone.
The landscape fell.

Azalea in Green Plastic

In this east window, snow
behind, this might be
summer in a pot, if
one imposed such meaning
on red shadows blooming so...

soaring and tumbling at once,
but decorously, a transparent
branchy lushness, saying
in an Oriental tongue:
                    "We remain temporary."

Black Cornish Horse

Surely more out of Mycenae, the kind
of creature that could be another
to amuse bored and imaginative tribes,
the half this and the half that,

this figure one of many waiting
to be kiln fired at a studio in Land's End
by a stringbean artist half-amused
we ask that he ship our selection to Canada—

pressed clay, fierce-faced and a child's delight,
hardly more than a curio, a souvenir of those days
when my expectations were heartily measured
with a stick calibrated for both low art and high.

That sodden July, Cornwall summed up best
just so, and now half this and half that surveys
the living room from the top of our mute piano.

my visual trope
(violet gillett's woodcut, the bus conductor)

All the players have seen the conductor
(the reason these figures gather
damply before this decked omnibus of storied
seating, all damp crosshatchings and trimly
etched angles, waiting to advance their wheeled
way to a vaulted destination, to decision and
precision), the elements colouring his stone-faced
facing figure in the peaked power cap—

witness the assured pose, his semaphored
arms at once beckoning and impeding,
all black and white and shade within shade
(that background figure lunging into the rain
might be any artist afoot, caught
in an act of contrived indifference
to our uniformed friend's authority).

There can be no proceeding without
he decides who's denied, who passes,
umbrellas furled (those curved stairs are clear,
a best unseen poetical foot edging
forward in anticipation),
                                    to ascension—
the misted view from atop.

This conductor writes the day,
plays to the gallery:
                            Fare, please.

REMEMBERING (PET)

They don't understand that
half-mast means two flag widths,
not halfway down the pole,
so this day jabber as they ready to hoist,
reckoning proper respect would keep it
as low as possible to the autumn ground.

One, the stumpier, a new Canadian
with an old accent, says
Why bother hook it on the lanyard, man,
he that dead.

IF YOU HAVE MONEY YOU'RE CLEVER AND HANDSOME, AND YOU CAN SING TOO

Nico's unspun memory of the Montreal poet
on the island of Mykonos...

> It was 1970,
> Westmount's Byron was strung out,
> not yet laconic,
> a vulpine consumer of Achaean women,
> wooing, in a black wind,
> a certain friend
>
> *I watched him treat her like shit,*
> recalls Nico
>
> *I would've knifed the bastard.*

Friends intervened.

The Yeshiva darkling retraced his salty steps.

The girl almost drowned in them.

> *Songs!*
>   *A wound still raw*
> *Poetry!*
>
> *Don't talk to me of L. Cohen!*

WELL, NOW THE STORY IS (JOSEPH'S ORANGES)

Well, now the story is
that Joseph, son of Jacob
grandson of Isaac
and great-grandson of Abraham
was so beautiful

so beautiful that his Egyptian master
Potiphar's wife languished
at his rejection

and because but a slave's rejection,
absent friends sensed only
that something was wrong

something to warrant
desperate measures
to demonstrate the why

and why Zuleika asked them
to her palace for bergamot tea
and the meatiest of oranges

blood-red oranges
nested in blue-veined bowls
and pledged to knives

the sharpest of fruit knives
with which each rich guest
might segment her gift

segment, but not notice
that when the slave made his entrance
each knife slipped

knives keen enough to cut
through the coil-springs of
magnetized hands, so that
beauty happened
                    in juice and blood

in blood and juice
her blooded friends saw
why she pined, why she bled
inside, though here were red
oranges served up by Joseph.

A PROSE POEM FOR HER DARK BIRTHDAY

The capital of our country is ominously bankrupt of sound, mechanic and ventricular. It is the first day past the height of the summer pennon's hanging, but so many shop windows are shut as to mimic the indifferent eyelid. Bleachers are being erected by sleepwalkers in preparation for a noble birthday fête. The very architecture of the celebrated institutions they face seems plastic, the stuff of souvenir gewgaws. Wry Daumier, his artwork housed on the banks of the Ottawa River, begins and remains richly elusive. At my every approach another lid descends. I miss the back-home boastfulness of Abegweit lupines, to which I am related by nature. Each day I hammer iron here, I ken that words are weightier than this site's quarried granite. It is the darkest hour of the night when I escape, in my clichéd celestial omnibus, from the susurrances of iconic fur and feather brushing into eternity the text of standing stone, moving east again to conflagrations contained within familiar chambers. Found at haven, a note from a wounded friend, herself gone invisible in transit, asking that I think of her in a time of new sorrow, knowing this needs no confirmation. I have flown between milestone and millstone, the shortest distance between two points of questionable embarkation.

stop me if you've heard this one

A Catholic priest, a Baptist minister
and a rabbi row into the centre of a lake,
where the Christian clerics engage
in rancorous disagreement
over the politics of theology.

The rabbi, keen to mediate, intervenes
and for his pains is pitched
into the water. A dreadful swimmer,
he calls out as he goes down for the last time,
"I was only trying to help!"

"That's your story," shouts the priest.
A large crucifix drifts by, buoyant,
"Climb on," calls the minister.
"I'd rather drown," the rabbi
responds, "than do that again."

HONSHU STREAM OF CONSCIOUSNESS
FOR HIROSHIMA MEMORIAL DAY

Some unanswerable questions, bald statements,
and vintage clichés:

How many times will we remember
before it is safe to forget?

How many born since 1945
to atone for those not born?

How, having split the atom, did
important people playing further
with fire become inevitable?

How can they be blamed
for a gormandizing curiosity, a lust
for limning Life large?

The eyes of those stamped young
bracket no memories, and few thoughts
of forces set free in the sky
above cities of the Divine Wind.

>   Which way does the wind blow
>   when the A-fuse is split?

Where are we taken? The map is greater,
the map has shriveled,
a fallen feather forces a thought.

Time's fireball, born ablaze above
our own island
would also ignite mythologies.

>   The hot god of war is omnivorous.

Small fires, smaller lights
assail a descending curtain
quilted with many eyelids.

In the end, does it matter
how we expire,
how we effect expiration?

Pain is surely unnecessary
once we have been warned.

What is horrific about the already horrific
being glossed and armed with new words
naming new names?

Fat Man, follow me up the stairs,
Little Boy, you've had a busy day.

      The Enola Gay had a stowaway;
      it was us.

If the blind are led by the blind,
where does the queue begin? Which
are the dancing masters, the disciples?

If we are not put on earth to ascend
and transcend, what purpose
but to cull or be culled?

Adjust your headset—
The portobello-shaped cloud recedes
in perceived importance, those beneath it
remaining nameless, the road-kill of war.

Let us remember verbs: Curie, Einstein,
Oppenheimer, the secrets of the atom
revealed... to beget more secrets.

death is deliverable in small packages.

> Quoth Walt Kelly: "We have seen the enemy
> and he is us."

I was born with the dawn-dusk of Japan-as-lab-rat,
feel responsible fifty-nine years later
for shedding only numerable tears,
for debating every debate,
with scant conviction.

Why whistle? Why sing?
No victory in the killing of one
child; but flags fly, men swear
to move in step, that the sun may
cloud their ashen faces.

And folks know better, mild
and wild, who ought to know best
why we dream the ideal, when
the ideal is an undone messiah,
heartless over Honshu.

MY BEAUTIFUL VEINS

Define me:
my nurses offer as much
in soft silence, utterances, smiles,
in the semi-regal fluttering
of their swallow hands,

once and again
as this needle and that needle
fall into the flesh (is it mine?),
delivering, taking away.

My beautiful veins
(and they are as described)
speak to health and facility
and swelling alacrity,

so let us get down to business:
smiles may become fleeting
with familiarity's onset, and
the work of hands and their time be
directed by a wind-challenged avian.

Conceit, conceit...

A hospital hums and shivers.
I would rather be beautiful than dead.

ROOTING AL PURDY

"There's nothing there any more...
it's gone from me,"
Pat Lane said he said,

for Al Purdy was twenty-four hours from dying
and in his eighty-second year—
ex-railrodder, airman, cab driver, mattress stuffer,
and self-styled bad rhyming poet until the advanced age of forty.

I am provoked to writing about him
by the invigorating sense of shared loss,
and the realization that Purdy won't read this.

And it's more than a tad ironic that he should
be the one to make it just this far,
until lung cancer hooked him fast,
as aged as he was big-boned and wiry—
but there it is.

His old compeers
Alden Nowlan and Milton Acorn
went down as youngsters,
especially Al Nowlan,
with whom Al Purdy used to tussle
about who'd had the hardest upbringing,
who had soonest been matriculated
at the school of hard knocks and the self-instructed,

devouring Holy Writ and Dickens,
Jane Austen and Zane Grey—
every imaginable literature
between covers, soft or hard,
and as much information, grand and trivial,
as could fit between such big ears
a hundred times over.

And I remember Purdy with his long arms, impossibly
angled, leaning into hotel-room corners
like an insouciant mantid,
some young beauty of a poet caught
 —ritually trapped—
between them,
                    me thinking, Purdy
you creaky cham, if you weren't so
hardworking famous
you'd never get near
those rippling tresses and rich perfumes;
she'd dash a league to be rid of you.

That nasal drawl and honk he offered up
that made you listen carefully or not at all
to what he pronounced and recited—
you might think the man was squiffy 24/7
(to use an expression Purdy'd employ only
to deride).

I went home from a festival reading one evening
with the woman who booed him
after he cracked wise about a broadcaster's panties,
in goat-tongued preamble to performing
one of his more sexist and engaging poems,

and nothing I could say then and now
would mitigate her reaction
to the cigar-chomping mantid
who was having far too much fun
acknowledging the life of Milton Acorn
while lustily living out his own.

And this was some years ago,
and Purdy's pal had been dead a decade—

Milton, who could be as conscious
of the spotlight and the camera
as any puffing *skald* who lurched across furrows—
so I imagine Purdy
as amused to be there,
maybe entertained
before the end.

Others will offer meaty anecdotes
about a complicated man who looked
anything but, and lanky besides,
but he had his own life
and a wife enduring
and a grown son in ill health
when he died,
so along with losing the poem
for the first and last time the day before,
he had tremendous cares,
if his head could contain them,

though the battle was done,
and he knew it with that admission—
something that would never have escaped him
had he remained a vital spirit
another day, his voice
more than the resigned noise breath makes
when it is expelled
once too often, and finally.

Remember this,
his moosey singsong about this country,
building entire poems from the textures of
names other people had conjured, invented,
appropriated and misappropriated:
Batoche and Pangnirtung, Nahanni, Namu,
Lilooet and Tulameen, Tuktoyaktuk,
Ameliasburg, Cariboo, Roblin's Mills, Roblin Lake,
and all the Annettes.

He loved sound as much as meaning,
the word as much as the geography.
It didn't matter who else camped there,
Purdy did. And he cleared the land,
and erected his houses of poetry.

He was a sadder man at the very end,
but not for long, not for very long,
so let's not linger there.
It couldn't be helped, as not much can.

Let's be complicit in this
and lie
          and say that his opus was completed
in painless sleep
where it and he remain.

Strange but true, we can agree,
Al Purdy has written another fine poem
and is keeping it to himself.

PRESCRIPTIVE

1.

I come to cats through dogs,
you come to cats through cats.
I ken this has made you a poet
for whom heedfulness orders
its own pulse, affording
exceptional accent, speaking
to the familiar and novel at once.

2.

                         The cat,
caught by a curved green lens,
leaping into the air
though catching nothing in its flight,
remains delighted
with its empty paws.

standard epigraphs redux

"In the genre of legend, all things are possible,
and exaggeration bears conviction. It is only in
this real world that the mud is heavy and sticks."
—Margaret Drabble, *The Witch of Exmoor*

Which is why,
when we turn away from the screen,
those images remain.

Don't shut your eyes,
it can only be worse.

Thousands of eyes follow us
through every room in the house.

Now there is mud, bled
upon a white carpet
we don't remember laying down.

"Ten lands are more easily known than
one man."
—Jewish Proverb

Relate for me ten known lands,
deal to me the mystery man
with his giocondo smile,

the shape of a weapon
swelling the great robe he wears
as a winding sheet.

"We ate our spaghetti that day with a sense of
high achievement, for who can see a great picture
or read a great book without taking some of the
credit for it himself...."
                              —John Bayley, *Elegy for Iris*

A moment ago
we were collectively God
of one bright mind

at the blue-skyed beginning
of our nice day,
the earth so distant below, yet

near enough to kiss,
to gravitate to
for a defining embrace.

Forgive me for believing
that's what we wanted.

"You can't roll the dice every day and
   not get waxed."
                     —Anonymous soldier in Paul Fussell's
                        Doing Battle: The Making of a Skeptic

Where was Superman?
That good Jewish boy
spent the Day of Atonement
expiating his own sins
not addressing those of others,
for he was never Jesus Christ.

For Taschlich he'd freed from his pockets
every possible crumb,
the river bearing his last year away.

The week before
he'd "read all about it"
in the *Daily Planet*
where he once daydreamt,
while tethered to his alias,
of leaping tall buildings
in a single bound,
of flying faster than a speeding bullet
if not a silvered thought.

Look, up in the sky!
Is it a bird? Is it a plane?

Man of Steel, descending.
Oh, Metropolis, metropolis.

PIRACY

I would make a truce with my body. You know
that with the sacked consciousness of the overnight
there might be rest for all embattled and assailed,
but in that dark passage something creeps along
on a simulacrum of a belly, with a blade between
its teeth, edging ever toward, its clinched smile
welding sharpness to sharpness, its smile that is
no smile. (And never a truce. Some end in mind.)

DILIGENT RIVER, ADVOCATE HARBOUR...

Such sober names.
Sober men and women settled this shore, made
earnest further by the sandless, fossil-rich stone
beach broken by time and geologic conglomeration.
One went to work with the brittle harshness ringing
the Minas Basin, shallow with a tidal heartbeat
that beat of extremes but not of time's effulgence—
this passage excavated by men.

Such diligent advocates.
Import. Export. Kindnesses would have to be painted
clear, with so much tolerable rawness configuring the scapes—
sea, land. There are small islands, near enough to suggest
the unlikely, circular enough to entrance the aware. Imagine,
in its day, a single boat, sail-fighting the wind and tide,
now charged and pushed by the noise it makes
into the mists and fish economy.

A wiry man, bent in the rain beside his kelp-line bungalow,
turns and pitches his coffee dregs at the blunt sea's edge,
barely registers the visitor a few metres along, who hugs the stony
illness he has brought with him and will take away, whispering
to himself about the found Cumberland, home of a human history
and of the igneous and a soup sea of lives committed
to this knuckled tidal basin. From his own Precambrian,
sober he comes and sober he goes, remarking in his own time.

AUGUST VISIT 2005

We've completed the ritual again,
motored northwest to cliff-defined
Cape Tryon (trespassing to do so)
and the familiar view from its heights,
the sea-paved way to Quebec.

A sea of a gleaned field, now an incline
that gives us pause, leads to topside and edge
and, viewing angle determined, the rock
formation sculpted by the elemental arsenal—
my sea serpent, its muzzle aimed at expansive waters.

But not this summer. What greets me
more resembles a prowed galleon in stone
(crewless, a ghost treasure ship?)
—some zoomorphic reversal.

Are the cape's cormorants safer for it?
Clouds of them define panic in the sun
as a bald eagle, cliff bound,
its breadth an amazement in glide,
dives at will to select.

We hike the short distance down,
leaving behind the unmanned galleon
without its serpentine roar, the seabirds
fearing the feathered and taloned known—
as I do.

CIVILIZATION

The red foxes are on the move
and nearer to town, astonishing
the patio mice,
the odd moony kitten—
cheeseburger wrappers glued
to their quivering bristles.

Quivering...

      The mouse-grey coyotes,
      loping wraiths,
      shadow their muttering,
      sidle in yellow-eyed conviction.

The sprung foxes
with unkempt brush
quiver with a sort of fear.

      Coyotes...

By way of explanation:
You too,
they say to those with ears,
will one day know them better.

about the author

Joseph Howard Sherman, CM, MA, was born in Bridgewater, Nova Scotia, in 1945, and raised in Whitney Pier, near Sydney, Cape Breton Island. He received his BA and MA from the University of New Brunswick, and taught English in Edmundston, New Brunswick, from 1970 to 1979. In 1979 he moved to Charlottetown, where he became the editor of the magazine, *ARTSatlantic*, through which he helped to bring vitality and a sense of identity to the region.

As the author of seven books of poetry, creator and curator of the Confederation Centre of the Arts' "Writing on the Wall" series, a founder of Saturday Morning Chapbooks, and a dedicated member of the League of Canadian Poets, Joe contributed immeasurably to the writing and artistic communities of Prince Edward Island, the Atlantic region, and Canada.

Joseph Sherman died on January 9, 2006, in Charlottetown.